WINE NOTES

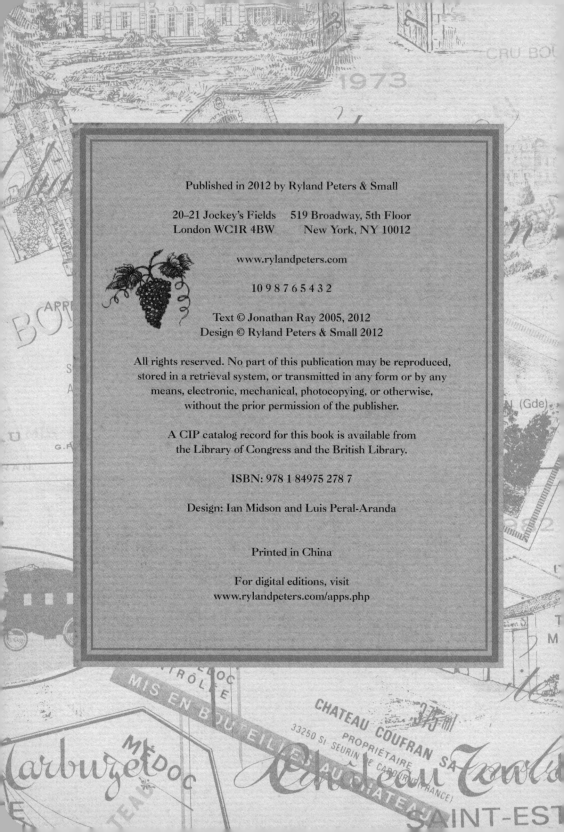

Published in 2012 by Ryland Peters & Small

20–21 Jockey's Fields   519 Broadway, 5th Floor
London WC1R 4BW   New York, NY 10012

www.rylandpeters.com

10 9 8 7 6 5 4 3 2

Text © Jonathan Ray 2005, 2012
Design © Ryland Peters & Small 2012

A CIP catalog record for this book is available from
the Library of Congress and the British Library.

ISBN: 978 1 84975 278 7

Design: Ian Midson and Luis Peral-Aranda

Printed in China

For digital editions, visit
www.rylandpeters.com/apps.php

CONTENTS

ENJOYING
WINE
AT HOME

HOW TO READ A WINE LABEL

Wine labels will give you all the information you need to make an informed decision about whether or not to buy the product. While front labels are strictly regulated, back labels often give a more detailed explanation of the wine. They might tell you which foods go well with the wine, what temperature it should be served at and so on.

OLD WORLD FRONT LABEL

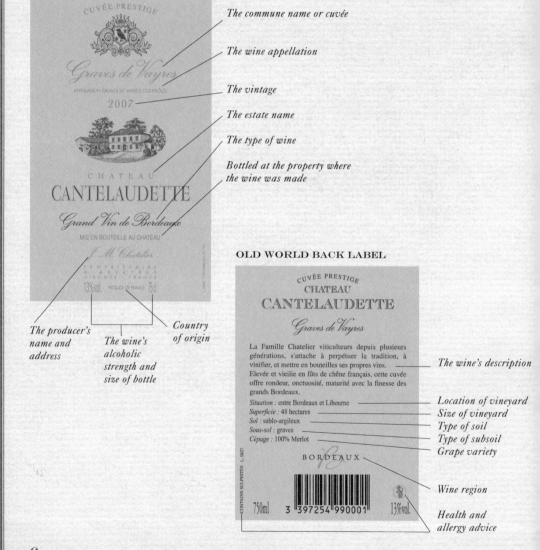

The commune name or cuvée

The wine appellation

The vintage

The estate name

The type of wine

Bottled at the property where the wine was made

The producer's name and address

The wine's alcoholic strength and size of bottle

Country of origin

OLD WORLD BACK LABEL

The wine's description

Location of vineyard

Size of vineyard

Type of soil

Type of subsoil

Grape variety

Wine region

Health and allergy advice

NEW WORLD FRONT LABEL

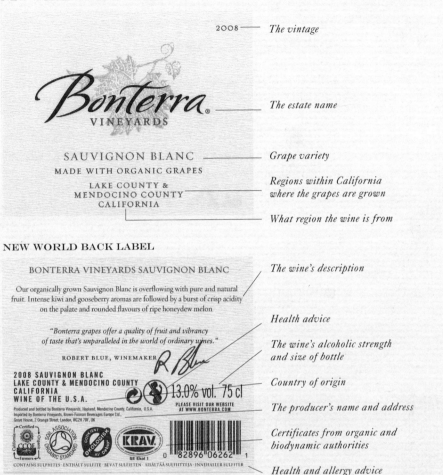

2008 —— *The vintage*

The estate name

SAUVIGNON BLANC —— *Grape variety*
MADE WITH ORGANIC GRAPES
LAKE COUNTY &
MENDOCINO COUNTY —— *Regions within California where the grapes are grown*
CALIFORNIA

What region the wine is from

NEW WORLD BACK LABEL

BONTERRA VINEYARDS SAUVIGNON BLANC —— *The wine's description*

Our organically grown Sauvignon Blanc is overflowing with pure and natural fruit. Intense kiwi and gooseberry aromas are followed by a burst of crisp acidity on the palate and rounded flavours of ripe honeydew melon.

"Bonterra grapes offer a quality of fruit and vibrancy of taste that's unparalleled in the world of ordinary wines."

ROBERT BLUE, WINEMAKER

Health advice

The wine's alcoholic strength and size of bottle

2008 SAUVIGNON BLANC
LAKE COUNTY & MENDOCINO COUNTY
CALIFORNIA —— *Country of origin*
WINE OF THE U.S.A.

13.0% vol. 75 cl

Produced and bottled by Bonterra Vineyards, Hopland, Mendocino County, California, U.S.A.
Imported by Bonterra Vineyards, Brown-Forman Beverages Europe Ltd.,
Grove House, 2 Orange Street, London, WC2H 7DF, UK —— *The producer's name and address*

PLEASE VISIT OUR WEBSITE AT WWW.BONTERRA.COM

Certificates from organic and biodynamic authorities

0 82896 06262 1

CONTAINS SULPHITES · ENTHÄLT SULFITE · BEVAT SULFIETEN · SISÄLTÄÄ SULFIITTEJA · INNEHÅLLER SULFITER —— *Health and allergy advice*

• New World producers tend to market their wines by grape variety, while the Europeans don't (although this is changing), so it helps to know which varieties make which wines.

• Wines sold within the EU require the words 'contains sulphites' if they were made using sulphur and 99.9% of them are. Wines sold in the US require this too, along with a warning from the surgeon general as to the hazards of drinking alcohol.

• Neck labels are sometimes added to a bottle. These might state the vintage or a special feature of the wine, or display an award won.

STORING WINE

BASIC GUIDELINES FOR STORING WINE AT HOME

Any space that is dark, free from vibrations and strong odours and that has an even temperature (neither too hot nor too cold) can be transformed into your own personal 'wine cellar'.

Places to avoid include kitchens (except for everyday wine) and rooms near garages and lift shafts, since cooking smells and diesel oil are surprisingly pervasive and vibrations can shake up sediment. Studies, cloakrooms and the cupboard under the stairs are ideal, as is the space under the bed in the spare room.

SELF-STORAGE

If you want more than just a cardboard wine box on its side, invest in some wine racks. These can be bought ready-made or custom built to fit the most unusual and awkward spaces in your home.

Temperature-controlled EuroCave wine cabinets are an excellent but expensive alternative if you have the money and the space. If price is no object, you can even have a steel tube containing a spiral cellar inserted into a hole dug into your drive or back garden.

TEMPERATURE

Wine likes to be cool, but isn't as fussy as people think. Between 10°C (50°F) and 15°C (59°F) is best, with 13°C (55°F) being the ideal. Much more important is maintaining a constant temperature and avoiding damp.

HOW TO STORE BOTTLES

Bottles should be laid on their sides to prevent the corks from drying out and shrinking. Fine wine in wooden cases should be left alone – the bottles will already be lying flat and, should you wish to sell them, unopened cases fetch a better price than opened ones.

IF YOU DON'T WANT TO OR CAN'T STORE WINE AT HOME

If you are investing in fine wine, then it is best either to store it with the merchant from whom you bought it or at independent, professionally run cellars. For a small annual fee (usually about £10 or $15 a year per dozen bottles), your wine will be kept in a perfect, temperature-controlled environment, making it easier to sell later on.

WINE EQUIPMENT

The number and quality of items of equipment and bar accessories you decide to buy will depend on how seriously you take the subject of wine.

• A corkscrew is essential, and it is important to get a good one. Although there are plenty to choose from – such as the 'waiter's friend' with a knife, the butterfly lever and the basic wooden-handled ones – none surpasses the Screwpull, which is easy to use and virtually infallible.

• Buy some foil cutters along with your corkscrew; they remove the top of the capsule in one easy twist, saving irritation and broken nails.

• If you are planning to decant your wines, you will need a decanter and a funnel. These need not be grand or expensive; a simple carafe and a plastic funnel are adequate. Keep a flashlight or candle handy for spotting the approaching sediment when decanting wine.

• Hot and cold sleeves – one for the microwave and one for the freezer – help bring a wine quickly to the correct serving temperature.

• Other useful accessories are a max/min thermometer for your cellar or cupboard under the stairs; stopper corks, or Vacuvins and wine preservers; a champagne stopper; an ice bucket and a wine cooler. A small basket is useful for transporting wine from the cellar to the table.

WINE GLASSES

If you are spending a considerable amount of money on some decent wine, it is worth investing in glasses that will allow the wine to be enjoyed at its best. There is no need to be faddy, but you will find that the right glass gives even the humblest wine a chance. Proper wine glasses are widely available and inexpensive. In an ideal world, you would have a choice of glasses for champagne and sparkling wines, white wines, red wines and fortified wines.

• Champagne should be served in tall flutes whose tapering rim helps retain the sparkle. Wide rimmed 'saucers' should not be used, because these allow the bubbles to dissipate far too quickly.

• Red and white wine should be served in glasses that are similar to each other but of different sizes: large for red and small for white. They should have stems – so that your hands do not affect the wine's temperature or obscure its appearance – and the bowl of the glass should be slightly wider than the rim so that you can swirl the liquid around without spilling it and without losing the wine's aroma.

• Dessert wines and fortified wines can be served in white wine glasses, although similar ones that are slightly smaller are better still.

• Plain, uncut, and uncolored glasses are ideal, giving the drinker a clear view of the wine. The better the glass, the lighter in weight it should be, and the easier to handle.

• Make sure your glasses do not become tainted by tastes or smells that might affect the wine. Wash them after each use with a light detergent and dry them with a clean cloth. Store your glasses upright in a cupboard, rather than face down, so that they don't get smells from the shelves trapped within them, or hang them upside down from a rack.

OPENING, DECANTING AND SERVING WINE

OPENING SPARKLING WINE
Remove the foil and wire, and hold the bottle at a slant with the base of the bottle in your strong hand and the cork in the other. Hold the cork firmly while slowly twisting the bottle, taking care not to shake it. Ease the cork out gently, covering it with the palm of your hand, while making sure you have a glass nearby in case the wine should froth out.

ICE BUCKETS AND COOLERS
If you are using an ice bucket, remember that plenty of water and a little ice will chill a bottle far more quickly and efficiently than plenty of ice and a little water. When using a wine cooler, bear in mind that it won't chill wine; it will simply keep the bottle at its starting temperature for a couple of hours, so make sure it is well-chilled in the fridge before serving.

DECANTING
There is no benefit in simply uncorking red wine hours before drinking – too little wine is exposed to the air to affect young wine, while the bouquet of old wine is apt to disappear. Far better to decant the wine, which rids an older wine of its sediment and gives a younger wine greater opportunity to 'breathe.' Even cheap wine is given a chance to show off. You don't have to use cut-glass decanters or silver funnels; a simple carafe – or even an empty, rinsed-out wine bottle – and a plastic funnel lined with filter-paper will do. If you are decanting without using filter-paper, pour the wine with a steady hand into the funnel, keeping an eye out for any sediment (a flashlight or candle is helpful here), and stop when the sediment reaches the neck.

SERVING TEMPERATURE

White wine should be cool enough to be refreshing, while red wine should be warm enough to exhibit its aroma and character. Ultimately, the temperature at which you serve a wine comes down to personal taste, so don't adhere too strictly to suggested levels – experience will tell you when you've got it right.

SUGGESTED TEMPERATURES FOR SERVING WHITE WINE

• 4–8°C (39–46°F) for everyday sparkling wine and dessert wine, Riesling and Vinho Verde.
• 8–11°C (46–52°F) for champagne, top-quality sparkling wine and dessert wine, Gewurztraminer, Viognier and rosé.
• 12–13°C (54–55°F) for top-quality Alsace, Chardonnay, Sauvignon and Sémillon.

SUGGESTED TEMPERATURES FOR SERVING RED WINE

• 10–13°C (50–55°F) for lighter reds such as Beaujolais, red Loire and Valpolicella.
• 14–16°C (57–61°F) for young red burgundy and Rhône, older claret, Chianti, Rioja and New World Pinot Noir.
• 16–18°C (61–64°F) for older burgundy, Rioja and Barolo, young claret and Rhône, and non-European Zinfandel, Cabernet, Merlot and Shiraz.

SERVING TIPS

• When pouring wine, serve yourself before your guests, so you catch any stray bits of cork that might be floating around.
• The rule of thumb when serving several wines is: dry before sweet, white before red, and young before old.
• When pouring wine in front of your guests, have the label pointing uppermost so they can see what they are drinking.

TASTING
WINE

RED GRAPE VARIETIES AND STYLES

VARIETIES

CABERNET SAUVIGNON
Key flavours Blackcurrant, mint, chocolate, tobacco, cedar wood, cigar box.
Identity Versatile, deep colour, high levels of tannin, good aging potential;
influenced by oak; best when blended with Merlot and Cabernet Franc.
Key regions Bordeaux in France, particularly in the Médoc when blended;
Australia, particularly Coonawarra, Victoria, and New South Wales, often
blended; Chile; USA, particularly Napa Valley; South Africa.

PINOT NOIR
Key flavours Violets, black cherry, aroma of the 'farmyard' (with age).
Identity Rich silky texture; most successful as a varietal; blended in
Champagne; influenced by oak; good aging potential; thin-skinned so light
in colour; delicate, high in acidity and low in tannin.
Key regions Burgundy in France, Champagne in France (blended with
Chardonnay and Pinot Meunier); New Zealand, particularly central Otago;
USA, particularly Oregon and Carneros, California; Australia, particularly
Victoria and Tasmania.

GAMAY
Key flavours Strawberry, bubble gum, banana.
Identity High in acidity, low in tannin, early drinking; dislikes oak, usually
a varietal.
Key regions Beaujolais in France, particularly the ten Beaujolais Crus.

ZINFANDEL
Key flavours Blackberry, blueberry, mixed spices.
Identity Juicy, high in alcohol, gets very ripe, high concentration of fruit,
dark colour.
Key regions California, particularly Sonoma; southern Italy (where it is
known as Primitivo).

MERLOT

Key flavours Ripe plums, coffee, black pepper.
Identity Low in acidity, soft in texture with low
tannin levels, juicy; usually blended with
Cabernet Sauvignon and Cabernet Franc;
influenced by oak; good aging for quality wines.
Key regions Bordeaux in France, particularly St.
Emilion and Pomerol when blended; California
and Washington State in the USA; Argentina;
Chile; New Zealand; South Africa.

CABERNET FRANC

Key flavours Raspberry, pencil shavings, tobacco, grass.
Identity Pale in colour, low in tannin, aromatic, high in acidity, light in
body; early drinking as a varietal; fine texture.
Key regions Bordeaux in France (blended with Cabernet Sauvignon and
Merlot); the Loire in France, particularly Chinon, St. Nicolas de Bourgeuil,
Saumur Champigny.

GRENACHE

Key flavours Raspberry, smoke, white pepper, aniseed, herbs.
Identity Usually part of a blend; high alcohol, low acidity; range of styles
from light to powerful wines depending on oak used.
Key regions Southern Rhône in France (blended with Cinsault, Mourvèdre,
Syrah), particularly Châteauneuf-du-Pape, Vacqueyras, Gigondas, Côtes
du Rhône; Languedoc-Roussillon in France for dry and sweet fortified;
Spain (where it is known as Garnacha), particularly Navarra; South
Australia.

SYRAH/SHIRAZ

Key flavours Redcurrant, black pepper, blackberry, tobacco, smoke.
Identity High in alcohol, high in tannin, moderate acidity; takes well to new
wood; varietal and blended; good aging qualities.
Key regions Northern Rhône in France, particularly Côte Rôtie and
Hermitage; Southern Rhône in France, particularly Châteauneuf-du-Pape

when blended; Australia, particularly Barossa Valley, Hunter Valley, and McLaren Vale; USA, particularly California and Washington State.

TEMPRANILLO
Key flavours Black cherry, vanilla, strawberry, tobacco.
Identity Moderate acidity and tannin; usually part of a blend; smooth and sweet-scented and delicate with age; likes American oak (vanilla flavour).
Key regions Spain, particularly Rioja, Ribera del Duero, Navarra.

SANGIOVESE
Key flavours Rose petals, cold tea, tar, black cherry, herbs.
Identity Moderate colour, medium-bodied, high in acidity and tannin; drink young; develops an orange rim with age.
Key regions Tuscany in Italy, particularly Chianti; California; Argentina.

NEBBIOLO
Key flavours Stewed prunes, cherry, truffle, leather, tar (with age).
Identity High acidity, tannin and alcohol; likes new oak; moderate colour.
Key regions Piedmont in Northern Italy, particularly Barolo and Barbaresco.

STYLES

LIGHT AND FRUITY REDS
Examples of grape varieties Gamay (for example, Beaujolais in France); Pinot Noir (for example, Burgundy in France and Sancerre Rouge from the Loire in France); Corvina (for example, Valpolicella from the Veneto in Italy); Dolcetto (for example, Dolcetto from Piedmont in Italy); Cabernet Franc (for example, Chinon, St. Nicholas de Bourgueil from the Loire in France).
Ideal with Pasta, pizza, fish, cold meats, salami, patés, picnics, barbecues.

SMOOTH AND MEDIUM-BODIED REDS
Examples of grape varieties Tempranillo (for example, Rioja in Spain); Syrah (for example, Crozes Hermitage from the Northern Rhône in France); Cabernet Sauvignon (for example, the South of France); Merlot (for example, Australia, California, Chile, South Africa, and the South of

France; Pinot Noir (for example,
Burgundy in France and California,
Australia and New Zealand); Sangiovese
(for example, Chianti from Tuscany in
Italy); blend of Grenache and Syrah (for
example, Côtes du Rhône in France);
blend of Cabernet Sauvignon and Merlot
(for example, Bordeaux in France).
Ideal with Mild-flavoured game
(pheasant, rabbit, quail, duck), pork,
veal, red meats, meat casseroles, poultry,
Camembert cheese (particularly well
matched to Pinot Noir).

FULL-BODIED REDS

Examples of grape varieties Syrah (for example, Cornas, Côte Rôtie, or
Hermitage from the Northern Rhône in France, and Shiraz from Australia
and New Zealand); Cabernet Sauvignon (for example, Australia, South
Africa, California and Chile); Nebbiolo (for example, Barolo from
Piedmont in Italy), Zinfandel (for example, California), Grenache and
Syrah blend (for example, Châteauneuf-du-Pape from the Southern Rhône
in France), Cabernet Sauvignon and Merlot blend (for example, Australia,
South Africa, California and Chile), Shiraz and Cabernet blend (for
example, Australia, South Africa, California and Chile).
Ideal with Stronger-flavoured game (hare, venison, pigeon), red meat such
as beef and lamb, hard strong-flavoured cheese.

ROSE WINES

Examples of grape varieties Cabernet Franc (for example, Rosé d'Anjou from
the Loire in France); Pinot Noir (for example, Sancerre Rosé from the
Loire in France); Grenache and Cinsault blend (for example, Tavel Rosé
from the Southern Rhône in France); Mourvèdre (for example, Provence
Rosé from the South of France).
Ideal with Pasta, pizza, fish, cold meats, ham, salami, patés, summer
picnics, barbecues.

WHITE GRAPE
VARIETIES AND STYLES

VARIETIES

CHARDONNAY

Key flavours Melon, butter, apple, pineapple, vanilla (if aged in oak), nuts.
Identity Adaptable: no pronounced characteristics of its own so takes on those of its environment; high in alcohol, moderate to high acidity, likes oak; best young except Burgundy.
Key regions Burgundy in France; Champagne in France (blended with Pinot Noir and Pinot Meunier); Australia; California; South Africa; New Zealand.

SAUVIGNON BLANC

Key flavours Gooseberry, asparagus, nettles.
Identity Aromatic, high acidity; often blended with Sémillon to provide dry and sweet styles; does not like oak except when blended; age only when blended.
Key regions The Loire in France, particularly Pouilly-Fumé and Sancerre; Bordeaux in France, particularly Péssac-Leognan when blended; New Zealand, particularly Marlborough; Chile; California.

CHENIN BLANC

Key flavours Dry: almond, lemon, green apple, damp straw, flowers. Sweet: honey, wet wool, beeswax, spice.
Identity High in acidity, does not like oak, high alcohol, pungent; wide range of styles; age sweeter styles and dry powerful styles only.
Key regions Dry: the Loire in France, particularly Savennières.
Sweet: the Loire, particularly Vouvray and Coteaux du Layon; California; South Africa.

SEMILLON

Key flavours Dry: lime, fig, cut grass, lemon, nectarine. Sweet: wax, honey, orange, toast.

Identity Heavy body, waxy texture, low acidity, high alcohol; often blended with Sauvignon Blanc to produce dry and sweet styles; does not like oak unless blended; age when blended; affected by noble rot.

Key regions Dry: Bordeaux in France, particularly Péssac-Leognan when blended; Australia, particularly Hunter Valley, Barossa Valley, and Western Australia. Sweet: Bordeaux in France, particularly Sauternes and Barsac when blended.

RIESLING

Key flavours Honeysuckle, rhubarb, apple, lime; gasoline, honey (with age).

Identity Low to medium alcohol, high acidity; does not like oak, particularly new oak; dry and late-harvested sweet styles; affected by noble rot; aromatic.

Key regions Germany, particularly Mosel, Pfalz, Nahe, Rheingau, Rheinhessen; Austria; Alsace in France; Australia; New Zealand; USA.

GEWURZTRAMINER

Key flavours Turkish delight, litchis, rose petals, spice.

Identity Very distinctive acquired taste, aromatic; low acidity and high alcohol gives an oily texture; does not like oak; age only sweet styles; sweet wines are late harvested; drink young.

Key regions Alsace in France.

VIOGNIER

Key flavours Peach, pear, apricot, nutmeg, cream.

Identity High in alcohol, low in acidity, rich texture, distinctive aromatic qualities; best enjoyed young.

Key regions Northern Rhône in France, particularly Condrieu; Languedoc-Roussillon in France; California; Australia.

MARSANNE

Key flavours Marzipan, almond.

Identity High in alcohol, low in acid; often blended with Roussanne; heaviness of texture on the palate.

Key regions Northern Rhône in France, particularly Hermitage; Australia; California.

MUSCAT

Key flavours Grape, orange blossom.

Identity Wide range of styles, mainly medium sweet to sweet; light and naturally low in alcohol; can be fortified.

Key regions Rhône in France, particularly Clairette de Die and sweet Vin Doux Naturel; northern Italy, particularly Moscato d'Asti and Asti Spumante; Australia, particularly Liqueur Muscat from Rutherglen, Victoria; California; South Africa.

STYLES

FRESH AND DRY WHITES

Examples of grape varieties Young Chenin Blanc (for example, from South Africa), Sauvignon Blanc (for example, Sancerre, Pouilly Fumé from the Loire in France), Chardonnay (for example, unoaked Chablis from France), Melon de Bourgogne (for example, Muscadet from the Loire in France).

Ideal with Salads, delicately flavoured fish, seafood pasta, oysters (particularly well matched with Chablis), seafood (particularly well matched with Muscadet), chicken dishes, goat cheese.

AROMATIC AND MEDIUM-DRY WHITES

Examples of grape varieties Riesling, Muscat, Viognier, Tokay Pinot Gris, Gewurztraminer, Chenin Blanc (for example, Vouvray from the Loire in France).

Ideal with Spicy Eastern flavours, foie gras (particularly well matched to Tokay Pinot Gris), soft cheese such as Camembert and Brie.

RICH AND FULL-BODIED WHITES

Examples of grape varieties Chardonnay (for example, from California, Chile, Australia, South Africa, and Burgundy in France); Viognier (for example, Condrieu from the Northern Rhône in France), Marsanne and Roussanne blend (for example, Hermitage from the Northern Rhône in France), Sauvignon Blanc and Sémillon blend (for example, Péssac-Leognan from Bordeaux in France).

Ideal with Fish such as turbot, lobster (particularly well matched to Chardonnays from California, Chile, Australia, and South Africa), oily fish such as mackerel and sardines, smoked salmon, crab, prawns/shrimp, scallops, poultry, particularly in sauces, pork and veal, creamy pasta.

SWEET WINES

Examples of grape varieties

Medium sweet Muscat (for example, Asti Spumante and Moscato from Piedmont in Italy); Riesling (for example, Auslese and Beerenauslese from Germany and vendange tardive from Alsace in France); Chenin Blanc (moelleux, for example, Coteaux du Layon from the Loire in France).

Sweet Muscat (for example, Vin Doux Naturel from the Rhône in France, and sweet Muscat from California);

Riesling (for example,
Trockenbeerenauslese from
Germany); Furmint (for example,
Tokaji from Hungary);
Gewurztraminer (for example,
vendange tardive from Alsace in
France); Sauvignon Blanc and
Sémillon blend (for example,
Sauternes or Barsac from
Bordeaux in France).

Very sweet Muscat (for example,
Australian Liqueur from
Rutherglen, Victoria).

Ideal with Desserts, foie gras,
blue cheese.

DESSERT WINES AND FORTIFIED WINES

The world's most celebrated dessert
wines come from Sauternes and
Barsac in Bordeaux, France, and from
Germany and Hungary, although fine
examples are also produced in Alsace,
Austria, Australia, California,
Canada, and Greece.

A dessert wine can be sweet for one of
several reasons. It might be a wine made
from very ripe grapes picked late in the
season when their sweetness is most
concentrated – known in France as vendange tardive – or it might be a vin doux
naturel such as Muscat de Beaumes-de-Venise, whose fermentation has been
stopped by adding brandy before all the sugar has turned to alcohol.

Alternatively, as in the case of a Sauternes or a Barsac, it might have
been made from grapes affected by noble rot, or botrytis cinerea. Botrytis
is a mold which, in areas prone to damp humid conditions, attacks certain
grapes, making them shrivel and rot, and concentrating their flavour and
their sugars in the process. Sauvignon Blanc, Sémillon, Gewurztraminer,
and Chenin Blanc in France, and Riesling in Germany are particularly
susceptible and – since the grapes are picked individually by hand – produce
dessert wines high in alcohol and rich in flavour.

Port is made by adding brandy to partly fermented red wine, which stops
its fermentation and leaves the wine sweet, rich, and high in alcohol. Madeira
is made in the same way, but is then baked to give it a rich caramel aroma.
Sercial and Verdelho are dry madeiras that make good aperitifs; Bual and
Malmsey are sweeter and go well with cookies and old-fashioned desserts.

Sherry is made in Spain from Moscatel, Palomino and Pedro Ximénez,
and fermented in barrels above ground – the wine gets its unique flavour from
'flor', a filmy growth that forms on its surface during fermentation. Manzanilla
and fino are the driest sherries and amontillado is medium dry. Cream sherry
is the sweetest, but it lacks the richness and fullness of flavour found in a
top-class oloroso, which can be dry or sweet to the taste.

CHAMPAGNE AND SPARKLING WINES

Even though 'bubbly' is now made all over the world, the only sparkling wine entitled to call itself champagne is made in the Champagne region of France by the reputable méthode champenoise. Other sparkling wines may be made from varieties such as Chenin Blanc, Muscat, Müller-Thurgau, Aligoté, Clairette, Riesling and Pinot Blanc, but champagne may be made only from Chardonnay and two red grapes, Pinot Noir and Pinot Meunier. The wine is generally dry and white, although sweet champagnes, rosé champagnes, and champagnes made solely from Chardonnay (known as blanc de blancs) or from a combination of Pinot Noir and Pinot Meunier (known as blanc de noirs) can also be found.

The vineyards of Champagne are the most northerly in France, and the grapes have difficulty ripening fully, leaving them high in acidity and low in flavour – ideal for winemakers seeking to achieve the austere, elegant styles characteristic of the best champagnes. Since biting frosts and hailstorms can affect the quality of each year's harvest, 80 per cent of production is devoted to non-vintage (NV) champagne – wines from different vintages blended to provide consistency in each producer's distinctive house style. The rarer vintage champagne is the wine of one outstanding year only.

HOW SPARKLERS ARE PRODUCED

According to the traditional méthode champenoise, grapes are picked and pressed, and the resulting juice undergoes an initial fermentation – usually in stainless-steel tanks, although some producers prefer to use oak barrels. Once fermented, the wines (which may be from different vintages, vineyards and grapes) are blended together. Before bottling,

an additional solution of yeast, sugar and wine (liqueur de tirage) is added, causing a second fermentation in the bottle, which produces the bubbles. Sealed with crown caps, the bottles mature on their sides for up to three years, after which they are regularly turned and gradually tilted – or riddled (remuage) – until they are vertical, causing the sediment created during the second fermentation to fall into the neck of the bottle. The necks are frozen, and the icy pellet of sediment is expelled by removing the cap – the pressure of the fizzy wine forces out the icy plug (dégorgement). Before corking and labelling, a mixture of wine and sugar (liqueur d'expédition) is introduced to the bottle (dosage).

Sparkling wines are made all over the world by méthode champenoise, with Germany, New Zealand, California, the Loire, Spain, Italy and Australia all producing excellent ones, usually from Chardonnay and Pinot Noir, although other grapes such as Riesling, Chenin Blanc and Aligoté are also used.

An alternative system – widely used in the New World – is the transfer method. Wines that have undergone their second fermentation in the bottle are disgorged under pressure into tanks – the whole contents, not just a frozen plug – before filtering and rebottling. The tank method, also known as the Cuve Close or the Charmat Process, involves a second fermentation in a sealed tank instead of a bottle; most German Sekt is made this way.

CHAMPAGNE BOTTLE SIZES

- Quarter bottle = 18.75ml (18.75cl)
- Half-bottle = 37.5ml (37.5cl)
- Bottle = 75ml (75cl)
- Magnum = 2 bottles
- Double magnum = 4 bottles
- Jeroboam = 4 bottles
- Rehoboam = 6 bottles
- Methuselah = 8 bottles
- Salmanazar = 12 bottles
- Balthazar = 16 bottles
- Nebuchadnezzar = 20 bottles

SOME OF THE BEST

Champagne is generally marketed under brand names. Among the best-known of these are Bollinger, Gosset, Jacquesson, Krug, Moët & Chandon, Mumm, Pol Roger, Louis Roederer, Ruinart, Salon, Taittinger and Veuve Clicquot. The desirable bubbly made elsewhere in France does not have such high-profile brand names, although high-quality regional wines are worth seeking out, such as Crémant d'Alsace, Crémant de Bourgogne from Burgundy, Blanquette de Limoux from Languedoc-Roussillon, sparkling Saumur and Vouvray from the Loire and Clairette de Die from near Grenoble.

Other European bubbly includes Cava from Spain; Sekt from Germany; and Prosecco, Franciacorta and the deliciously sweet Asti from Italy. But the biggest revolution in sparkling wine has occurred in the New World, with wonderful méthode champenoise bubbly now being produced, including Quartet and Mumm Cuvée Napa from California, Pelorus from New Zealand, and the Australian-made Seaview and Taltarni.

WINE WORDS

Acidity A feature of wine – natural acids give wine character and structure, and help it age.

Aerate Bring a wine into contact with air to accelerate its development.

Alcohol Sugar in ripe grapes turns into alcohol to produce wine

Aroma Varietal smell of a wine.

Balance A wine's harmonious combination of acids, tannins, alcohol, fruit and flavour.

Bereich (German) Wine-producing district.

Bianco (Italian) White.

Blanc (French) White.

Blanc de blancs (French) White wine made only from white grapes.

Blanc de noirs (French) White wine made only from black (red) grapes.

Blanco (Spanish) White.

Blend Mixture of more than one grape variety.

Blind tasting Wine tasting at which labels and shapes of bottles are concealed from tasters.

Bodega (Spanish) Winery.

Body Weight and structure of a wine.

Botrytis cinerea Fungus that shrivels and rots white grapes, concentrating their flavours and sugars; creates dessert wines high in alcohol and rich in flavour. Also known as noble rot, pourriture noble and edelfäule.

Bouquet Complex scent of a wine that develops as it matures.

Cantina (Italian) Winery or cellar.

Cave (French) Cellar.

Cepa (Spanish) Vine variety.

Cépage (French) Vine variety.

Chai (French) Place for storing wine.

Chambrer (French) Allow a wine gradually to reach room temperature before drinking it.

Château (French) Wine-growing property – used chiefly in Bordeaux.

Claret Red wine of Bordeaux.

Clos (French) Enclosed vineyard.

Colheita (Portuguese) Vintage; also used to denote a single vintage port.

Complex (said of a wine) Marked by a variety of flavours.

Concentrated (said of a wine) Marked by depth, richness, and fruitiness.

Core Colour of wine in the center of a glass.

Corkage Charge per bottle levied on customers in restaurants who bring in their own wine to drink.

Corked Condition, revealed by a musty odour, where a wine has been contaminated by a faulty cork.

Cosecha (Spanish) Vintage.

Côte (French) Hillside of vineyards.

Crémant (French) Semi-sparkling.

Cru (French) Growth or vineyard.

Cru Classé (French) Classed Growth,

especially 61 red wines of the Médoc (and one from the Graves) in Bordeaux graded into five categories according to price in 1855. Similar classifications followed elsewhere in Bordeaux for Graves red wines in 1953 and for St. Emilion in 1954 (revised 1969 and 1985).

Cuvée (French) Blended wine or special selection.

Demi-sec (French) Semisweet.

Dolce (Italian) Sweet.

Domaine (French) Property or estate.

Doux (French) Sweet.

Dulce (Spanish) Sweet.

Extract Concentration of fruit in a wine.

Fermentation Transformation of grape juice into wine, whereby yeasts – naturally present in grapes and occasionally added in cultured form – convert sugars into alcohol.

Finesse Complexity and subtlety in a wine.

Flavour Aroma and taste of a wine, compared to fruits, spices, and so on.

Fortified wine Wine – such as port, sherry, or madeira – to which alcohol has been added either to stop it from fermenting before all its sugars turn to alcohol or simply to strengthen it.

Frizzante (Italian) Semi-sparkling.

Full-bodied (said of wine) Marked by a high level of fruit concentration and alcohol.

Grand cru (French) Top-quality wines from Alsace, Bordeaux, Burgundy and Champagne.

Halbtrocken (German) Medium dry.

Horizontal tasting Tasting of several different wines all from the same vintage.

Integrated (said of wine) Where tannins in a wine are harmonious with the other components of the wine.

Jahrgang (German) Vintage.

Keller (German) Cellar.

Landwein (German) A level of quality wine just above simple table wine, equivalent to the French vin de pays.

Late harvest (said of grapes) Very ripe grapes that have been picked late when their sweetness is most concentrated.

Legs Thickness left on the inside of the glass by some wines.

Length (said of wine) How long the taste of a wine lasts after it has been swallowed or spat out.

Meritage Term coined in 1988 for California wines blended from the classic red varieties of Bordeaux.

Méthode champenoise Method by which champagnes and top-quality sparkling wines are made; involves a secondary fermentation in bottle.

Moelleux (French) Sweet.

Mousse (French) Effervescence in a glass of sparkling wine as it is poured.

Mousseux (French) Sparkling.

Négociant (French) Wine merchant, shipper, or grower who buys wine or grapes in bulk from several sources before vinifying and/or bottling the wine himself.

Noble rot Botrytis cinera fungus, which attacks grape skins and results in super-concentration.

Non-vintage (NV) A wine that is a blend of more than one vintage, notably champagne.

Nose The qualities of a wine that create the sensation experienced by smelling it. This is not just a matter of the wine's scent; the nose also conveys information about the wine's wellbeing.

Oak Wine aged in oak barrels can be identified by whiffs of vanilla or cedarwood.

Oxidized (said of wine) Wine that has deteriorated as a result of its overexposure to air.

Palate Taste of a wine in the mouth.

Perlant (French) Very faintly sparkling.

Perlwein (German) A type of low-grade semi-sparkling wine.

Pétillant (French) Slightly sparkling.

Phylloxera Aphidlike insect that attacks the roots of grapevines with disastrous results.

Punt Indentation at the bottom of a bottle which catches any sediment and strengthens the bottle.

Quinta (Portuguese) Wine-growing estate.

Récolte (French) Crop or vintage.

Rich (said of wine) With a good concentration of ripe fruit.

Rosso (Italian) Red.

Rouge (French) Red.

Sec (French) Dry.

Secco (Italian) Dry.

Seco (Spanish/Portuguese) Dry.

Sediment Deposit that forms after a wine has spent a long time in a bottle.

Sekt (German) Sparkling wine.

Smooth (said of wine) With good fruit levels and soft integrated tannins.

Soft (said of wine) Rounded, fruity and low in tannin.

Sparkling (said of wine) Produced to have bubbles.

Spritzer Refreshing drink made from white wine and club soda or sparkling spring water, and often served with ice.

Spumante (Italian) Sparkling.

Sulfur Pungent smell given off by wine that can be dispersed by swirling the glass.

Sur lie (said of wine) Aged on its lees or sediment before bottling – resulting in a greater depth of flavour.

Sweetness A quality of wine created by unfermented sugar deriving from the ripeness of the grapes.

Tannin Austere acid found in some

red wines, usually young ones, deriving from grape skins and stalks combined with the oak barrels in which the wine has been aged; it is a necessary preservative.

Tafelwien (German) Table wine.

Tartrates Harmless crystals that can be found in both red and white wines.

Tastevin A small silver tasting dish, most commonly used in Burgundy.

Tears Thickness left on the inside of the glass by some wines.

Terroir (French) Meaning literally 'soil' or 'earth', terroir encompasses climate, drainage, position, and anything else that distinguishes the taste of a wine from that of its immediate neighbors which have been grown and produced in the same way.

Texture What a wine feels like in the mouth; it is often compared to the feel of fabrics.

Tinto (Spanish/Portuguese) Red.

Trocken (German) Dry.

Ullage Amount of air in a bottle or barrel between the top of the wine and the base of the cork or bung.

Varietal Wine named after the grape (or the major constituent grape) from which it is made.

Variety Breed of grape.

Vendange (French) Harvest or vintage.

Vendange tardive (French) Late harvest.

Vendemmia (Italian) Harvest or vintage.

Vendimia (Spanish) Harvest or vintage.

Vertical tasting Tasting of several wines from the same property that are all from different vintages.

Vigneron (French) Wine grower.

Vin de pays (French) Country wine of a level higher than table wine.

Vin de table (French) Table wine.

Vin doux naturel (VDN) (French) Fortified wine that has been sweetened and strengthened by the addition of alcohol, either before or after fermentation.

Vin ordinaire (French) Basic wine not subject to any regulations.

Vinification Winemaking.

Vino da tavola (Italian) Table wine.

Vino de mesa (Spanish) Table wine.

Vintage Year of a grape harvest and the wine made from the grapes of that harvest.

Viscosity Thickness in a wine with a great density of fruit extract and alcohol – indicated by 'tears' or 'legs' on the side of the glass.

Viticulture Cultivation of grapes.

Weight Body and/or strength of a wine.

Winery Winemaking establishment.

Use these pages to record impressions of each wine you taste, comparing for example, various vintages from the same winemaker.

TASTING NOTES

WINE & VINTAGE   *Date of tasting*

Winemaker

Country & region

Where & when purchased   *Price*

Colour & clarity

Bouquet

Taste

Finish

Other comments

WINE & VINTAGE   *Date of tasting*

Winemaker

Country & region

Where & when purchased   *Price*

Colour & clarity

Bouquet

Taste

Finish

Other comments

TASTING NOTES

WINE & VINTAGE   *Date of tasting*

Winemaker

Country & region

Where & when purchased   *Price*

Colour & clarity

Bouquet

Taste

Finish

Other comments

WINE & VINTAGE   *Date of tasting*

Winemaker

Country & region

Where & when purchased   *Price*

Colour & clarity

Bouquet

Taste

Finish

Other comments

TASTING NOTES

WINE & VINTAGE

Date of tasting

Winemaker

Country & region

Where & when purchased   *Price*

Colour & clarity

Bouquet

Taste

Finish

Other comments

WINE & VINTAGE

Date of tasting

Winemaker

Country & region

Where & when purchased   *Price*

Colour & clarity

Bouquet

Taste

Finish

Other comments

TASTING NOTES

WINE & VINTAGE
Date of tasting

Winemaker

Country & region

Where & when purchased
Price

Colour & clarity

Bouquet

Taste

Finish

Other comments

WINE & VINTAGE
Date of tasting

Winemaker

Country & region

Where & when purchased
Price

Colour & clarity

Bouquet

Taste

Finish

Other comments

TASTING NOTES

WINE & VINTAGE *Date of tasting*

Winemaker

Country & region

Where & when purchased *Price*

Colour & clarity

Bouquet

Taste

Finish

Other comments

WINE & VINTAGE *Date of tasting*

Winemaker

Country & region

Where & when purchased *Price*

Colour & clarity

Bouquet

Taste

Finish

Other comments

TASTING NOTES

WINE & VINTAGE   *Date of tasting*

Winemaker

Country & region

Where & when purchased   *Price*

Colour & clarity

Bouquet

Taste

Finish

Other comments

WINE & VINTAGE   *Date of tasting*

Winemaker

Country & region

Where & when purchased   *Price*

Colour & clarity

Bouquet

Taste

Finish

Other comments

TASTING NOTES

WINE & VINTAGE *Date of tasting*

Winemaker

Country & region

Where & when purchased *Price*

Colour & clarity

Bouquet

Taste

Finish

Other comments

WINE & VINTAGE *Date of tasting*

Winemaker

Country & region

Where & when purchased *Price*

Colour & clarity

Bouquet

Taste

Finish

Other comments

TASTING NOTES

WINE & VINTAGE *Date of tasting*

Winemaker

Country & region

Where & when purchased *Price*

Colour & clarity

Bouquet

Taste

Finish

Other comments

WINE & VINTAGE *Date of tasting*

Winemaker

Country & region

Where & when purchased *Price*

Colour & clarity

Bouquet

Taste

Finish

Other comments

TASTING NOTES

WINE & VINTAGE   *Date of tasting*

Winemaker

Country & region

Where & when purchased   *Price*

Colour & clarity

Bouquet

Taste

Finish

Other comments

WINE & VINTAGE   *Date of tasting*

Winemaker

Country & region

Where & when purchased   *Price*

Colour & clarity

Bouquet

Taste

Finish

Other comments

TASTING NOTES

WINE & VINTAGE   *Date of tasting*

Winemaker

Country & region

Where & when purchased   *Price*

Colour & clarity

Bouquet

Taste

Finish

Other comments

WINE & VINTAGE   *Date of tasting*

Winemaker

Country & region

Where & when purchased   *Price*

Colour & clarity

Bouquet

Taste

Finish

Other comments

TASTING NOTES

WINE & VINTAGE

Date of tasting

Winemaker

Country & region

Where & when purchased

Price

Colour & clarity

Bouquet

Taste

Finish

Other comments

WINE & VINTAGE

Date of tasting

Winemaker

Country & region

Where & when purchased

Price

Colour & clarity

Bouquet

Taste

Finish

Other comments

TASTING NOTES

WINE & VINTAGE *Date of tasting*

Winemaker

Country & region

Where & when purchased *Price*

Colour & clarity

Bouquet

Taste

Finish

Other comments

WINE & VINTAGE *Date of tasting*

Winemaker

Country & region

Where & when purchased *Price*

Colour & clarity

Bouquet

Taste

Finish

Other comments

TASTING NOTES

WINE & VINTAGE

Date of tasting

Winemaker

Country & region

Where & when purchased

Price

Colour & clarity

Bouquet

Taste

Finish

Other comments

WINE & VINTAGE

Date of tasting

Winemaker

Country & region

Where & when purchased

Price

Colour & clarity

Bouquet

Taste

Finish

Other comments

TASTING NOTES

WINE & VINTAGE
Date of tasting

Winemaker

Country & region

Where & when purchased
Price

Colour & clarity

Bouquet

Taste

Finish

Other comments

WINE & VINTAGE
Date of tasting

Winemaker

Country & region

Where & when purchased
Price

Colour & clarity

Bouquet

Taste

Finish

Other comments

TASTING NOTES

WINE & VINTAGE   Date of tasting

Winemaker

Country & region

Where & when purchased   Price

Colour & clarity

Bouquet

Taste

Finish

Other comments

WINE & VINTAGE   Date of tasting

Winemaker

Country & region

Where & when purchased   Price

Colour & clarity

Bouquet

Taste

Finish

Other comments

TASTING NOTES

WINE & VINTAGE   *Date of tasting*

Winemaker

Country & region

Where & when purchased   *Price*

Colour & clarity

Bouquet

Taste

Finish

Other comments

WINE & VINTAGE   *Date of tasting*

Winemaker

Country & region

Where & when purchased   *Price*

Colour & clarity

Bouquet

Taste

Finish

Other comments

TASTING NOTES

WINE & VINTAGE *Date of tasting*

Winemaker

Country & region

Where & when purchased *Price*

Colour & clarity

Bouquet

Taste

Finish

Other comments

WINE & VINTAGE *Date of tasting*

Winemaker

Country & region

Where & when purchased *Price*

Colour & clarity

Bouquet

Taste

Finish

Other comments

TASTING NOTES

WINE & VINTAGE *Date of tasting*

Winemaker

Country & region

Where & when purchased *Price*

Colour & clarity

Bouquet

Taste

Finish

Other comments

WINE & VINTAGE *Date of tasting*

Winemaker

Country & region

Where & when purchased *Price*

Colour & clarity

Bouquet

Taste

Finish

Other comments

TASTING NOTES

WINE & VINTAGE   *Date of tasting*

Winemaker

Country & region

Where & when purchased   *Price*

Colour & clarity

Bouquet

Taste

Finish

Other comments

WINE & VINTAGE   *Date of tasting*

Winemaker

Country & region

Where & when purchased   *Price*

Colour & clarity

Bouquet

Taste

Finish

Other comments

TASTING NOTES

WINE & VINTAGE   *Date of tasting*

Winemaker

Country & region

Where & when purchased   *Price*

Colour & clarity

Bouquet

Taste

Finish

Other comments

WINE & VINTAGE   *Date of tasting*

Winemaker

Country & region

Where & when purchased   *Price*

Colour & clarity

Bouquet

Taste

Finish

Other comments

TASTING NOTES

WINE & VINTAGE *Date of tasting*

Winemaker

Country & region

Where & when purchased *Price*

Colour & clarity

Bouquet

Taste

Finish

Other comments

WINE & VINTAGE *Date of tasting*

Winemaker

Country & region

Where & when purchased *Price*

Colour & clarity

Bouquet

Taste

Finish

Other comments

TASTING NOTES

WINE & VINTAGE   *Date of tasting*

Winemaker

Country & region

Where & when purchased   *Price*

Colour & clarity

Bouquet

Taste

Finish

Other comments

WINE & VINTAGE   *Date of tasting*

Winemaker

Country & region

Where & when purchased   *Price*

Colour & clarity

Bouquet

Taste

Finish

Other comments

TASTING NOTES

WINE & VINTAGE *Date of tasting*

Winemaker

Country & region

Where & when purchased *Price*

Colour & clarity

Bouquet

Taste

Finish

Other comments

WINE & VINTAGE *Date of tasting*

Winemaker

Country & region

Where & when purchased *Price*

Colour & clarity

Bouquet

Taste

Finish

Other comments

TASTING NOTES

WINE & VINTAGE   *Date of tasting*

Winemaker

Country & region

Where & when purchased   *Price*

Colour & clarity

Bouquet

Taste

Finish

Other comments

WINE & VINTAGE   *Date of tasting*

Winemaker

Country & region

Where & when purchased   *Price*

Colour & clarity

Bouquet

Taste

Finish

Other comments

TASTING NOTES

WINE & VINTAGE   *Date of tasting*

Winemaker

Country & region

Where & when purchased   *Price*

Colour & clarity

Bouquet

Taste

Finish

Other comments

WINE & VINTAGE   *Date of tasting*

Winemaker

Country & region

Where & when purchased   *Price*

Colour & clarity

Bouquet

Taste

Finish

Other comments

TASTING NOTES

WINE & VINTAGE   *Date of tasting*

Winemaker

Country & region

Where & when purchased   *Price*

Colour & clarity

Bouquet

Taste

Finish

Other comments

WINE & VINTAGE   *Date of tasting*

Winemaker

Country & region

Where & when purchased   *Price*

Colour & clarity

Bouquet

Taste

Finish

Other comments

TASTING NOTES

WINE & VINTAGE   *Date of tasting*

Winemaker

Country & region

Where & when purchased   *Price*

Colour & clarity

Bouquet

Taste

Finish

Other comments

WINE & VINTAGE   *Date of tasting*

Winemaker

Country & region

Where & when purchased   *Price*

Colour & clarity

Bouquet

Taste

Finish

Other comments

TASTING NOTES

WINE & VINTAGE   *Date of tasting*

Winemaker

Country & region

Where & when purchased   *Price*

Colour & clarity

Bouquet

Taste

Finish

Other comments

WINE & VINTAGE   *Date of tasting*

Winemaker

Country & region

Where & when purchased   *Price*

Colour & clarity

Bouquet

Taste

Finish

Other comments

TASTING NOTES

WINE & VINTAGE

Date of tasting

Winemaker

Country & region

Where & when purchased

Price

Colour & clarity

Bouquet

Taste

Finish

Other comments

WINE & VINTAGE

Date of tasting

Winemaker

Country & region

Where & when purchased

Price

Colour & clarity

Bouquet

Taste

Finish

Other comments

TASTING NOTES

WINE & VINTAGE   *Date of tasting*

Winemaker

Country & region

Where & when purchased   *Price*

Colour & clarity

Bouquet

Taste

Finish

Other comments

WINE & VINTAGE   *Date of tasting*

Winemaker

Country & region

Where & when purchased   *Price*

Colour & clarity

Bouquet

Taste

Finish

Other comments

TASTING NOTES

WINE & VINTAGE

Date of tasting

Winemaker

Country & region

Where & when purchased

Price

Colour & clarity

Bouquet

Taste

Finish

Other comments

WINE & VINTAGE

Date of tasting

Winemaker

Country & region

Where & when purchased

Price

Colour & clarity

Bouquet

Taste

Finish

Other comments

TASTING NOTES

WINE & VINTAGE *Date of tasting*

Winemaker

Country & region

Where & when purchased *Price*

Colour & clarity

Bouquet

Taste

Finish

Other comments

WINE & VINTAGE *Date of tasting*

Winemaker

Country & region

Where & when purchased *Price*

Colour & clarity

Bouquet

Taste

Finish

Other comments

TASTING NOTES

WINE & VINTAGE

Date of tasting

Winemaker

Country & region

Where & when purchased

Price

Colour & clarity

Bouquet

Taste

Finish

Other comments

WINE & VINTAGE

Date of tasting

Winemaker

Country & region

Where & when purchased

Price

Colour & clarity

Bouquet

Taste

Finish

Other comments

TASTING NOTES

WINE & VINTAGE   *Date of tasting*

Winemaker

Country & region

Where & when purchased   *Price*

Colour & clarity

Bouquet

Taste

Finish

Other comments

WINE & VINTAGE   *Date of tasting*

Winemaker

Country & region

Where & when purchased   *Price*

Colour & clarity

Bouquet

Taste

Finish

Other comments

TASTING NOTES

WINE & VINTAGE   *Date of tasting*

Winemaker

Country & region

Where & when purchased   *Price*

Colour & clarity

Bouquet

Taste

Finish

Other comments

WINE & VINTAGE   *Date of tasting*

Winemaker

Country & region

Where & when purchased   *Price*

Colour & clarity

Bouquet

Taste

Finish

Other comments

TASTING NOTES

WINE & VINTAGE   *Date of tasting*

Winemaker

Country & region

Where & when purchased   *Price*

Colour & clarity

Bouquet

Taste

Finish

Other comments

WINE & VINTAGE   *Date of tasting*

Winemaker

Country & region

Where & when purchased   *Price*

Colour & clarity

Bouquet

Taste

Finish

Other comments

TASTING NOTES

WINE & VINTAGE

Date of tasting

Winemaker

Country & region

Where & when purchased

Price

Colour & clarity

Bouquet

Taste

Finish

Other comments

WINE & VINTAGE

Date of tasting

Winemaker

Country & region

Where & when purchased

Price

Colour & clarity

Bouquet

Taste

Finish

Other comments

TASTING NOTES

WINE & VINTAGE
Date of tasting

Winemaker

Country & region

Where & when purchased
Price

Colour & clarity

Bouquet

Taste

Finish

Other comments

WINE & VINTAGE
Date of tasting

Winemaker

Country & region

Where & when purchased
Price

Colour & clarity

Bouquet

Taste

Finish

Other comments

TASTING NOTES

WINE & VINTAGE *Date of tasting*

Winemaker

Country & region

Where & when purchased *Price*

Colour & clarity

Bouquet

Taste

Finish

Other comments

WINE & VINTAGE *Date of tasting*

Winemaker

Country & region

Where & when purchased *Price*

Colour & clarity

Bouquet

Taste

Finish

Other comments

TASTING NOTES

WINE & VINTAGE   *Date of tasting*

Winemaker

Country & region

Where & when purchased   *Price*

Colour & clarity

Bouquet

Taste

Finish

Other comments

WINE & VINTAGE   *Date of tasting*

Winemaker

Country & region

Where & when purchased   *Price*

Colour & clarity

Bouquet

Taste

Finish

Other comments

TASTING NOTES

WINE & VINTAGE

Date of tasting

Winemaker

Country & region

Where & when purchased

Price

Colour & clarity

Bouquet

Taste

Finish

Other comments

WINE & VINTAGE

Date of tasting

Winemaker

Country & region

Where & when purchased

Price

Colour & clarity

Bouquet

Taste

Finish

Other comments

TASTING NOTES

WINE & VINTAGE

Date of tasting

Winemaker

Country & region

Where & when purchased

Price

Colour & clarity

Bouquet

Taste

Finish

Other comments

WINE & VINTAGE

Date of tasting

Winemaker

Country & region

Where & when purchased

Price

Colour & clarity

Bouquet

Taste

Finish

Other comments

TASTING NOTES

WINE & VINTAGE   *Date of tasting*

Winemaker

Country & region

Where & when purchased   *Price*

Colour & clarity

Bouquet

Taste

Finish

Other comments

WINE & VINTAGE   *Date of tasting*

Winemaker

Country & region

Where & when purchased   *Price*

Colour & clarity

Bouquet

Taste

Finish

Other comments

TASTING NOTES

WINE & VINTAGE

Date of tasting

Winemaker

Country & region

Where & when purchased   *Price*

Colour & clarity

Bouquet

Taste

Finish

Other comments

WINE & VINTAGE

Date of tasting

Winemaker

Country & region

Where & when purchased   *Price*

Colour & clarity

Bouquet

Taste

Finish

Other comments

TASTING NOTES

WINE & VINTAGE _Date of tasting_

Winemaker

Country & region

Where & when purchased _Price_

Colour & clarity

Bouquet

Taste

Finish

Other comments

WINE & VINTAGE _Date of tasting_

Winemaker

Country & region

Where & when purchased _Price_

Colour & clarity

Bouquet

Taste

Finish

Other comments

TASTING NOTES

WINE & VINTAGE _Date of tasting_

Winemaker

Country & region

Where & when purchased _Price_

Colour & clarity

Bouquet

Taste

Finish

Other comments

WINE & VINTAGE _Date of tasting_

Winemaker

Country & region

Where & when purchased _Price_

Colour & clarity

Bouquet

Taste

Finish

Other comments

Use these pages to create a lasting record of
events at which you drank memorable wines.

SPECIAL OCCASIONS

OCCASION   *Date*

Guests

Food

Wine

Comments

SPECIAL OCCASIONS

OCCASION   Date

Guests

Food

Wine

Comments

SPECIAL OCCASIONS

OCCASION   *Date*

Guests

Food

Wine

Comments

SPECIAL OCCASIONS

OCCASION   *Date*

Guests

Food

Wine

Comments

SPECIAL OCCASIONS

OCCASION   *Date*

Guests

Food

Wine

Comments

SPECIAL OCCASIONS

OCCASION   *Date*

Guests

Food

Wine

Comments

SPECIAL OCCASIONS

OCCASION _Date_

Guests

Food

Wine

Comments

SPECIAL OCCASIONS

OCCASION *Date*

Guests

Food

Wine

Comments

SPECIAL OCCASIONS

OCCASION   *Date*

Guests

Food

Wine

Comments

SPECIAL OCCASIONS

OCCASION   *Date*

Guests

Food

Wine

Comments

SPECIAL OCCASIONS

OCCASION _Date_

Guests

Food

Wine

Comments

SPECIAL OCCASIONS

OCCASION   *Date*

Guests

Food

Wine

Comments

SPECIAL OCCASIONS

OCCASION _Date_

Guests

Food

Wine

Comments

SPECIAL OCCASIONS

OCCASION *Date*

Guests

Food

Wine

Comments

SPECIAL OCCASIONS

OCCASION   Date

Guests

Food

Wine

Comments

SPECIAL OCCASIONS

OCCASION   *Date*

Guests

Food

Wine

Comments

Use these pages to note any details of wines that have been enjoyed and recommended to you by others.

RECOMMENDATIONS

RECOMMENDER

Wine & vintage

Winemaker

Country & region

Where & when purchased

Price

Recommender's comments

Your own comments

Date of tasting

RECOMMENDER

Wine & vintage

Winemaker

Country & region

Where & when purchased

Price

Recommender's comments

Your own comments

Date of tasting

RECOMMENDATIONS

RECOMMENDER

Wine & vintage

Winemaker

Country & region

Where & when purchased

Price

Recommender's comments

Your own comments

Date of tasting

RECOMMENDER

Wine & vintage

Winemaker

Country & region

Where & when purchased

Price

Recommender's comments

Your own comments

Date of tasting

RECOMMENDATIONS

RECOMMENDER

Wine & vintage

Winemaker

Country & region

Where & when purchased

Price

Recommender's comments

Your own comments

Date of tasting

RECOMMENDER

Wine & vintage

Winemaker

Country & region

Where & when purchased

Price

Recommender's comments

Your own comments

Date of tasting

RECOMMENDATIONS

RECOMMENDER

Wine & vintage

Winemaker

Country & region

Where & when purchased

Price

Recommender's comments

Your own comments

Date of tasting

RECOMMENDER

Wine & vintage

Winemaker

Country & region

Where & when purchased

Price

Recommender's comments

Your own comments

Date of tasting

RECOMMENDATIONS

RECOMMENDER

Wine & vintage

Winemaker

Country & region

Where & when purchased

Price

Recommender's comments

Your own comments

Date of tasting

RECOMMENDER

Wine & vintage

Winemaker

Country & region

Where & when purchased

Price

Recommender's comments

Your own comments

Date of tasting

RECOMMENDATIONS

RECOMMENDER

Wine & vintage

Winemaker

Country & region

Where & when purchased

Price

Recommender's comments

Your own comments

Date of tasting

RECOMMENDER

Wine & vintage

Winemaker

Country & region

Where & when purchased

Price

Recommender's comments

Your own comments

Date of tasting

RECOMMENDATIONS

RECOMMENDER

Wine & vintage

Winemaker

Country & region

Where & when purchased

Price

Recommender's comments

Your own comments

Date of tasting

RECOMMENDER'S

Wine & vintage

Winemaker

Country & region

Where & when purchased

Price

Recommender's comments

Your own comments

Date of tasting

RECOMMENDATIONS

RECOMMENDER

Wine & vintage

Winemaker

Country & region

Where & when purchased

Price

Recommender's comments

Your own comments

Date of tasting

RECOMMENDER

Wine & vintage

Winemaker

Country & region

Where & when purchased

Price

Recommender's comments

Your own comments

Date of tasting

RECOMMENDATIONS

RECOMMENDER
Wine & vintage

Winemaker

Country & region

Where & when purchased

Price

Recommender's comments

Your own comments

Date of tasting

RECOMMENDER
Wine & vintage

Winemaker

Country & region

Where & when purchased

Price

Recommender's comments

Your own comments

Date of tasting

RECOMMENDATIONS

RECOMMENDER

Wine & vintage

Winemaker

Country & region

Where & when purchased

Price

Recommender's comments

Your own comments

Date of tasting

RECOMMENDER

Wine & vintage

Winemaker

Country & region

Where & when purchased

Price

Recommender's comments

Your own comments

Date of tasting

RECOMMENDATIONS

RECOMMENDER

Wine & vintage

Winemaker

Country & region

Where & when purchased

Price

Recommender's comments

Your own comments

Date of tasting

RECOMMENDER

Wine & vintage

Winemaker

Country & region

Where & when purchased

Price

Recommender's comments

Your own comments

Date of tasting

RECOMMENDATIONS

RECOMMENDER

Wine & vintage

Winemaker

Country & region

Where & when purchased

Price

Recommender's comments

Your own comments

Date of tasting

RECOMMENDER

Wine & vintage

Winemaker

Country & region

Where & when purchased

Price

Recommender's comments

Your own comments

Date of tasting

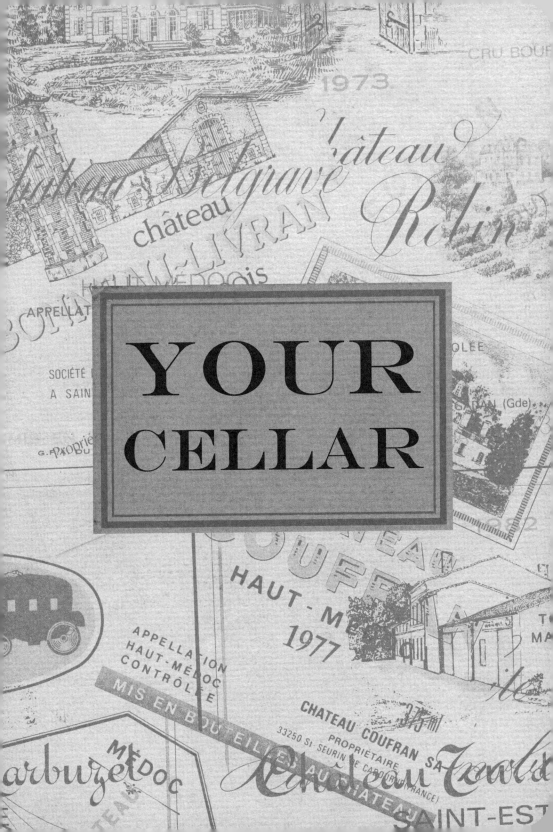

YOUR CELLAR

PLANNING YOUR CELLAR

It has never been easier to buy wine. Ordinary reds, whites and sparkling wines can be bought when required from supermarkets – but fully mature fine wine is both hard to find and quite often prohibitively expensive. If you want to drink quality wine of some age, the only sensible option is to mature it yourself by laying it down.

Wine for everyday drinking is not intended to be laid down – rather than maturing, it simply loses its fruit and vivacity. There is no point in cluttering up your cellar with wines that you can get easily and cheaply elsewhere or with wines that will not improve. Instead, seek out wines of quality, rarity, and aging potential.

Start by buying what you like to drink. You need also to decide whether your wines are for consumption or investment, or both. Some smart wine-lovers buy two cases of each wine, one to drink and one to sell. This way, after the initial investment, a cellar can become self-financing. Keep up to date with what's happening in the world of wine by joining suppliers' mailing lists, looking on the internet, and reading specialist wine magazines as well as newspaper columnists who write about wine.

Consistent and favourable climates in the Americas, South Africa and Australasia, as well as increasingly sophisticated technology in Europe's wine-growing areas, mean that really poor vintages are a thing of the past, but there can still be huge variations between years, and age alone does not define a good wine. Don't restrict your wine buying to just one vintage or your cellar will lack variety, and you may find that the style of a subsequent vintage is more to your taste. Remember, too, that different vintages age at different rates, and that later vintages are sometimes ready to drink before earlier ones.

Tastes and budgets differ, and no two cellars will be alike, but a notional well-balanced cellar might include several bottles of Cabernet and Merlot, red and white burgundy, and Rhône for the long term, plus a couple of bottles of vintage champagne and vintage port and some half-bottles of dessert wine. For the short term, there might be some white wines from the Loire and some mid-range wines from California, Chile or New Zealand.

CABERNET SAUVIGNON AND MERLOT

Top-quality wines made from Cabernet Sauvignon demand to be laid down, whether they are the finest single varietals from California, Australia, Chile and Italy, or the subtle blended wines from Bordeaux known as clarets. Wines made from Merlot also merit time in the cellar, although they will mature more quickly than their Cabernet counterparts.

PINOT NOIR

Although Pinot Noir ages well, its most sought-after wines, such as those from New Zealand, Oregon and Burgundy are now usually made for early consumption. Investing in burgundy can be both simple and confusing: simple because all red burgundies are made from one grape – Pinot Noir – and confusing because wines of the same name but from different producers proliferate. It is vital, therefore, either to get to know names of producers you like or to find a specialized supplier whom you trust.

SHIRAZ, GRENACHE AND ZINFANDEL

Wines made from Shiraz – also known as Syrah – and from Grenache are ideal to lay down. Both varieties produce wines of great power, with abundant fruit and plenty of tannin, perfect for lengthy maturation. The best examples are the blockbuster Shirazes from Australia and the Syrah-based northern Rhônes and the Grenache-based southern Rhônes from France, all of which are much prized by collectors. Keep an eye out, too, for the best California Zinfandels.

CHARDONNAY AND VIOGNIER

Chardonnay is the best of all white grape varieties to lay down. Choose the finest examples from Australia, California, Burgundy and Chablis. Oak-aged Chardonnay, in particular, matures well, taking on deep yellow hues and rich toasty and buttery aromas as the years pass. Serious wines made from Viognier are also worth making space for in your cellar.

SAUVIGNON BLANC

As a rule, wines made from Sauvignon Blanc don't age well – if kept for too long, they lose their zest. Notable exceptions are the powerful dessert wines blended from Sauvignon Blanc and Sémillon, which benefit from lengthy storage. For short-term cellaring, have some good-quality California or New Zealand Sauvignons or some Sancerres or Pouilly Fumés from the Loire.

CHAMPAGNE AND SPARKLING WINES

Vintage champagne (made in exceptional years only) is ideal for maturing, as are the finest New World sparkling wines made from the classic Chardonnay/Pinot Noir blend. Good-quality non-vintage champagne (produced every year) can be laid down over a couple of years to let its acidity soften and mellow.

DESSERT WINE

Dessert wines are well worth keeping, be they the great Sauvignon/Sémillon blends of Sauternes and Barsac, the sumptuous vendanges tardives of Alsace, the intense Riesling Trockenbeerenauslesen of Germany, or the unique Tokajis of Hungary. A little dessert wine goes a long way, so buy it in half-bottles.

PORT

There are two main types of port: wood and vintage. Wood port is aged in cask; since it is mature once bottled, there is no point in cellaring it. Vintage port is made only three or four times a decade and spends only a short time in cask before lengthy maturation in bottle. This is the type of port to lay down.

- Often, the best way to buy fine wine is when it is offered en primeur – where, each spring following the vintage, producers reveal the opening price for their new wine as they make their allocations to wine merchants.
- Buying wine at auction can be fun and yield bargains – but find out the wine's provenance, since long-term bad storage can spoil even the best wine.
- Buying wine 'in bond' allows you to delay paying tax and duty until you are ready to take delivery, months or years later.

MISCELLANEOUS

Other wines to consider are top Riojas from Spain, Italy's super vini da tavola and hefty Italian wines such as Barolo and Barbaresco. Australia and California are producing full-bodied red wines and big Chardonnays that repay keeping.

SHERRY AND SPIRITS

Fino and manzanilla sherries must be drunk promptly to enjoy their zippy freshness, but olorosos can develop a pleasing nuttiness over time. There is no point in storing spirits – however grand or illustrious a bottle of brandy or single malt whisky might be, it won't improve with age.

111

*Use these pages to record details of wine you have laid
down – either as an investment or for future enjoyment*

STORED WINE

WINE & VINTAGE

Winemaker

Country & region

Where & when purchased   *Price*

Quantity & bottle size

Estimated date of maturity

Location

Comments

WINE & VINTAGE

Winemaker

Country & region

Where & when purchased   *Price*

Quantity & bottle size

Estimated date of maturity

Location

Comments

STORED WINE

WINE & VINTAGE _____

Winemaker _____

Country & region _____

Where & when purchased _____ *Price* _____

Quantity & bottle size _____

Estimated date of maturity _____

Location _____

Comments _____

_____

_____

_____

_____

WINE & VINTAGE _____

Winemaker _____

Country & region _____

Where & when purchased _____ *Price* _____

Quantity & bottle size _____

Estimated date of maturity _____

Location _____

Comments _____

_____

_____

_____

_____

STORED WINE

WINE & VINTAGE

Winemaker

Country & region

Where & when purchased   *Price*

Quantity & bottle size

Estimated date of maturity

Location

Comments

WINE & VINTAGE

Winemaker

Country & region

Where & when purchased   *Price*

Quantity & bottle size

Estimated date of maturity

Location

Comments

STORED WINE

WINE & VINTAGE

Winemaker

Country & region

Where & when purchased   *Price*

Quantity & bottle size

Estimated date of maturity

Location

Comments

WINE & VINTAGE

Winemaker

Country & region

Where & when purchased   *Price*

Quantity & bottle size

Estimated date of maturity

Location

Comments

STORED WINE

WINE & VINTAGE

Winemaker

Country & region

Where & when purchased   *Price*

Quantity & bottle size

Estimated date of maturity

Location

Comments

WINE & VINTAGE

Winemaker

Country & region

Where & when purchased   *Price*

Quantity & bottle size

Estimated date of maturity

Location

Comments

STORED WINE

WINE & VINTAGE

Winemaker

Country & region

Where & when purchased   *Price*

Quantity & bottle size

Estimated date of maturity

Location

Comments

WINE & VINTAGE

Winemaker

Country & region

Where & when purchased   *Price*

Quantity & bottle size

Estimated date of maturity

Location

Comments

STORED WINE

WINE & VINTAGE

Winemaker

Country & region

Where & when purchased   *Price*

Quantity & bottle size

Estimated date of maturity

Location

Comments

WINE & VINTAGE

Winemaker

Country & region

Where & when purchased   *Price*

Quantity & bottle size

Estimated date of maturity

Location

Comments

STORED WINE

WINE & VINTAGE
_____

Winemaker
_____

Country & region
_____

Where & when purchased   _Price_
_____

Quantity & bottle size
_____

Estimated date of maturity
_____

Location
_____

Comments
_____
_____
_____
_____
_____

WINE & VINTAGE
_____

Winemaker
_____

Country & region
_____

Where & when purchased   _Price_
_____

Quantity & bottle size
_____

Estimated date of maturity
_____

Location
_____

Comments
_____
_____
_____
_____
_____

STORED WINE

WINE & VINTAGE

Winemaker

Country & region

Where & when purchased   *Price*

Quantity & bottle size

Estimated date of maturity

Location

Comments

WINE & VINTAGE

Winemaker

Country & region

Where & when purchased   *Price*

Quantity & bottle size

Estimated date of maturity

Location

Comments

STORED WINE

WINE & VINTAGE

Winemaker

Country & region

Where & when purchased   *Price*

Quantity & bottle size

Estimated date of maturity

Location

Comments

WINE & VINTAGE

Winemaker

Country & region

Where & when purchased   *Price*

Quantity & bottle size

Estimated date of maturity

Location

Comments

STORED WINE

WINE & VINTAGE

Winemaker

Country & region

Where & when purchased   *Price*

Quantity & bottle size

Estimated date of maturity

Location

Comments

WINE & VINTAGE

Winemaker

Country & region

Where & when purchased   *Price*

Quantity & bottle size

Estimated date of maturity

Location

Comments

STORED WINE

WINE & VINTAGE

Winemaker

Country & region

Where & when purchased   *Price*

Quantity & bottle size

Estimated date of maturity

Location

Comments

WINE & VINTAGE

Winemaker

Country & region

Where & when purchased   *Price*

Quantity & bottle size

Estimated date of maturity

Location

Comments

STORED WINE

WINE & VINTAGE

Winemaker

Country & region

Where & when purchased   *Price*

Quantity & bottle size

Estimated date of maturity

Location

Comments

WINE & VINTAGE

Winemaker

Country & region

Where & when purchased   *Price*

Quantity & bottle size

Estimated date of maturity

Location

Comments

STORED WINE

WINE & VINTAGE

Winemaker

Country & region

Where & when purchased   *Price*

Quantity & bottle size

Estimated date of maturity

Location

Comments

WINE & VINTAGE

Winemaker

Country & region

Where & when purchased   *Price*

Quantity & bottle size

Estimated date of maturity

Location

Comments

STORED WINE

WINE & VINTAGE

Winemaker

Country & region

Where & when purchased   *Price*

Quantity & bottle size

Estimated date of maturity

Location

Comments

WINE & VINTAGE

Winemaker

Country & region

Where & when purchased   *Price*

Quantity & bottle size

Estimated date of maturity

Location

Comments

STORED WINE

WINE & VINTAGE

Winemaker

Country & region

Where & when purchased   *Price*

Quantity & bottle size

Estimated date of maturity

Location

Comments

WINE & VINTAGE

Winemaker

Country & region

Where & when purchased   *Price*

Quantity & bottle size

Estimated date of maturity

Location

Comments

STORED WINE

WINE & VINTAGE

Winemaker

Country & region

Where & when purchased   *Price*

Quantity & bottle size

Estimated date of maturity

Location

Comments

WINE & VINTAGE

Winemaker

Country & region

Where & when purchased   *Price*

Quantity & bottle size

Estimated date of maturity

Location

Comments

STORED WINE

WINE & VINTAGE

Winemaker

Country & region

Where & when purchased   *Price*

Quantity & bottle size

Estimated date of maturity

Location

Comments

WINE & VINTAGE

Winemaker

Country & region

Where & when purchased   *Price*

Quantity & bottle size

Estimated date of maturity

Location

Comments

STORED WINE

WINE & VINTAGE

Winemaker

Country & region

Where & when purchased   *Price*

Quantity & bottle size

Estimated date of maturity

Location

Comments

WINE & VINTAGE

Winemaker

Country & region

Where & when purchased   *Price*

Quantity & bottle size

Estimated date of maturity

Location

Comments

STORED WINE

WINE & VINTAGE

Winemaker

Country & region

Where & when purchased   *Price*

Quantity & bottle size

Estimated date of maturity

Location

Comments

WINE & VINTAGE

Winemaker

Country & region

Where & when purchased   *Price*

Quantity & bottle size

Estimated date of maturity

Location

Comments

STORED WINE

WINE & VINTAGE

Winemaker

Country & region

Where & when purchased   *Price*

Quantity & bottle size

Estimated date of maturity

Location

Comments

WINE & VINTAGE

Winemaker

Country & region

Where & when purchased   *Price*

Quantity & bottle size

Estimated date of maturity

Location

Comments

STORED WINE

WINE & VINTAGE

Winemaker

Country & region

Where & when purchased　　　　　　　　　　*Price*

Quantity & bottle size

Estimated date of maturity

Location

Comments

WINE & VINTAGE

Winemaker

Country & region

Where & when purchased　　　　　　　　　　*Price*

Quantity & bottle size

Estimated date of maturity

Location

Comments

STORED WINE

WINE & VINTAGE

Winemaker

Country & region

Where & when purchased   *Price*

Quantity & bottle size

Estimated date of maturity

Location

Comments

WINE & VINTAGE

Winemaker

Country & region

Where & when purchased   *Price*

Quantity & bottle size

Estimated date of maturity

Location

Comments

STORED WINE

WINE & VINTAGE _____

Winemaker _____

Country & region _____

Where & when purchased _____ *Price* _____

Quantity & bottle size _____

Estimated date of maturity _____

Location _____

Comments _____

_____

_____

_____

_____

WINE & VINTAGE _____

Winemaker _____

Country & region _____

Where & when purchased _____ *Price* _____

Quantity & bottle size _____

Estimated date of maturity _____

Location _____

Comments _____

_____

_____

_____

_____

STORED WINE

WINE & VINTAGE

Winemaker

Country & region

Where & when purchased   *Price*

Quantity & bottle size

Estimated date of maturity

Location

Comments

WINE & VINTAGE

Winemaker

Country & region

Where & when purchased   *Price*

Quantity & bottle size

Estimated date of maturity

Location

Comments

STORED WINE

WINE & VINTAGE

Winemaker

Country & region

Where & when purchased   *Price*

Quantity & bottle size

Estimated date of maturity

Location

Comments

WINE & VINTAGE

Winemaker

Country & region

Where & when purchased   *Price*

Quantity & bottle size

Estimated date of maturity

Location

Comments

STORED WINE

WINE & VINTAGE
_____

Winemaker
_____

Country & region
_____

Where & when purchased   _Price_
_____

Quantity & bottle size
_____

Estimated date of maturity
_____

Location
_____

Comments
_____

_____

_____

_____

_____

WINE & VINTAGE
_____

Winemaker
_____

Country & region
_____

Where & when purchased   _Price_
_____

Quantity & bottle size
_____

Estimated date of maturity
_____

Location
_____

Comments
_____

_____

_____

_____

STORED WINE

WINE & VINTAGE

Winemaker

Country & region

Where & when purchased   *Price*

Quantity & bottle size

Estimated date of maturity

Location

Comments

WINE & VINTAGE

Winemaker

Country & region

Where & when purchased   *Price*

Quantity & bottle size

Estimated date of maturity

Location

Comments

STORED WINE

WINE & VINTAGE

Winemaker

Country & region

Where & when purchased   *Price*

Quantity & bottle size

Estimated date of maturity

Location

Comments

WINE & VINTAGE

Winemaker

Country & region

Where & when purchased   *Price*

Quantity & bottle size

Estimated date of maturity

Location

Comments

STORED WINE

WINE & VINTAGE
_____

Winemaker
_____

Country & region
_____

Where & when purchased   _Price_
_____

Quantity & bottle size
_____

Estimated date of maturity
_____

Location
_____

Comments
_____

_____

_____

_____

_____

_____

WINE & VINTAGE
_____

Winemaker
_____

Country & region
_____

Where & when purchased   _Price_
_____

Quantity & bottle size
_____

Estimated date of maturity
_____

Location
_____

Comments
_____

_____

_____

_____

_____

STORED WINE

WINE & VINTAGE

Winemaker

Country & region

Where & when purchased   *Price*

Quantity & bottle size

Estimated date of maturity

Location

Comments

WINE & VINTAGE

Winemaker

Country & region

Where & when purchased   *Price*

Quantity & bottle size

Estimated date of maturity

Location

Comments

STORED WINE

WINE & VINTAGE

Winemaker

Country & region

Where & when purchased   *Price*

Quantity & bottle size

Estimated date of maturity

Location

Comments

WINE & VINTAGE

Winemaker

Country & region

Where & when purchased   *Price*

Quantity & bottle size

Estimated date of maturity

Location

Comments

STORED WINE

WINE & VINTAGE

Winemaker

Country & region

Where & when purchased   *Price*

Quantity & bottle size

Estimated date of maturity

Location

Comments

WINE & VINTAGE

Winemaker

Country & region

Where & when purchased   *Price*

Quantity & bottle size

Estimated date of maturity

Location

Comments

STORED WINE

WINE & VINTAGE

Winemaker

Country & region

Where & when purchased   *Price*

Quantity & bottle size

Estimated date of maturity

Location

Comments

WINE & VINTAGE

Winemaker

Country & region

Where & when purchased   *Price*

Quantity & bottle size

Estimated date of maturity

Location

Comments

STORED WINE

WINE & VINTAGE
_____

Winemaker
_____

Country & region
_____

Where & when purchased   _Price_
_____

Quantity & bottle size
_____

Estimated date of maturity
_____

Location
_____

Comments
_____
_____
_____
_____
_____

WINE & VINTAGE
_____

Winemaker
_____

Country & region
_____

Where & when purchased   _Price_
_____

Quantity & bottle size
_____

Estimated date of maturity
_____

Location
_____

Comments
_____
_____
_____
_____
_____

STORED WINE

WINE & VINTAGE

Winemaker

Country & region

Where & when purchased   *Price*

Quantity & bottle size

Estimated date of maturity

Location

Comments

WINE & VINTAGE

Winemaker

Country & region

Where & when purchased   *Price*

Quantity & bottle size

Estimated date of maturity

Location

Comments

STORED WINE

WINE & VINTAGE

Winemaker

Country & region

Where & when purchased   *Price*

Quantity & bottle size

Estimated date of maturity

Location

Comments

WINE & VINTAGE

Winemaker

Country & region

Where & when purchased   *Price*

Quantity & bottle size

Estimated date of maturity

Location

Comments

STORED WINE

WINE & VINTAGE

Winemaker

Country & region

Where & when purchased   *Price*

Quantity & bottle size

Estimated date of maturity

Location

Comments

WINE & VINTAGE

Winemaker

Country & region

Where & when purchased   *Price*

Quantity & bottle size

Estimated date of maturity

Location

Comments

STORED WINE

WINE & VINTAGE

Winemaker

Country & region

Where & when purchased   *Price*

Quantity & bottle size

Estimated date of maturity

Location

Comments

WINE & VINTAGE

Winemaker

Country & region

Where & when purchased   *Price*

Quantity & bottle size

Estimated date of maturity

Location

Comments

STORED WINE

WINE & VINTAGE

Winemaker

Country & region

Where & when purchased   _Price_

Quantity & bottle size

Estimated date of maturity

Location

Comments

WINE & VINTAGE

Winemaker

Country & region

Where & when purchased   _Price_

Quantity & bottle size

Estimated date of maturity

Location

Comments

STORED WINE

WINE & VINTAGE

Winemaker

Country & region

Where & when purchased   *Price*

Quantity & bottle size

Estimated date of maturity

Location

Comments

WINE & VINTAGE

Winemaker

Country & region

Where & when purchased   *Price*

Quantity & bottle size

Estimated date of maturity

Location

Comments

STORED WINE

WINE & VINTAGE _____

Winemaker _____

Country & region _____

Where & when purchased _____ *Price* _____

Quantity & bottle size _____

Estimated date of maturity _____

Location _____

Comments _____

_____

_____

_____

_____

WINE & VINTAGE _____

Winemaker _____

Country & region _____

Where & when purchased _____ *Price* _____

Quantity & bottle size _____

Estimated date of maturity _____

Location _____

Comments _____

_____

_____

_____

_____

STORED WINE

WINE & VINTAGE

Winemaker

Country & region

Where & when purchased   Price

Quantity & bottle size

Estimated date of maturity

Location

Comments

WINE & VINTAGE

Winemaker

Country & region

Where & when purchased   Price

Quantity & bottle size

Estimated date of maturity

Location

Comments

STORED WINE

WINE & VINTAGE

Winemaker

Country & region

Where & when purchased   Price

Quantity & bottle size

Estimated date of maturity

Location

Comments

WINE & VINTAGE

Winemaker

Country & region

Where & when purchased   Price

Quantity & bottle size

Estimated date of maturity

Location

Comments

*Use these pages to record details of wines that you
have stored short-term for everyday drinking.*

EVERYDAY WINE

WINE & VINTAGE

Winemaker

Country & region

Where & when purchased   *Price*

Quantity & bottle size

Location

Comments

WINE & VINTAGE

Winemaker

Country & region

Where & when purchased   *Price*

Quantity & bottle size

Location

Comments

EVERYDAY WINE

WINE & VINTAGE

Winemaker

Country & region

Where & when purchased   Price

Quantity & bottle size

Location

Comments

WINE & VINTAGE

Winemaker

Country & region

Where & when purchased   Price

Quantity & bottle size

Location

Comments

EVERYDAY WINE

WINE & VINTAGE

Winemaker

Country & region

Where & when purchased   *Price*

Quantity & bottle size

Location

Comments

WINE & VINTAGE

Winemaker

Country & region

Where & when purchased   *Price*

Quantity & bottle size

Location

Comments

EVERYDAY WINE

WINE & VINTAGE

Winemaker

Country & region

Where & when purchased   *Price*

Quantity & bottle size

Location

Comments

WINE & VINTAGE

Winemaker

Country & region

Where & when purchased   *Price*

Quantity & bottle size

Location

Comments

EVERYDAY WINE

WINE & VINTAGE

Winemaker

Country & region

Where & when purchased   *Price*

Quantity & bottle size

Location

Comments

WINE & VINTAGE

Winemaker

Country & region

Where & when purchased   *Price*

Quantity & bottle size

Location

Comments

EVERYDAY WINE

WINE & VINTAGE

Winemaker

Country & region

Where & when purchased   *Price*

Quantity & bottle size

Location

Comments

WINE & VINTAGE

Winemaker

Country & region

Where & when purchased   *Price*

Quantity & bottle size

Location

Comments

EVERYDAY WINE

WINE & VINTAGE

Winemaker

Country & region

Where & when purchased   *Price*

Quantity & bottle size

Location

Comments

WINE & VINTAGE

Winemaker

Country & region

Where & when purchased   *Price*

Quantity & bottle size

Location

Comments

EVERYDAY WINE

WINE & VINTAGE

Winemaker

Country & region

Where & when purchased   *Price*

Quantity & bottle size

Location

Comments

WINE & VINTAGE

Winemaker

Country & region

Where & when purchased   *Price*

Quantity & bottle size

Location

Comments

EVERYDAY WINE

WINE & VINTAGE
_____

Winemaker
_____

Country & region
_____

Where & when purchased   _Price_
_____

Quantity & bottle size
_____

Location
_____

Comments
_____

_____

_____

_____

_____

WINE & VINTAGE
_____

Winemaker
_____

Country & region
_____

Where & when purchased   _Price_
_____

Quantity & bottle size
_____

Location
_____

Comments
_____

_____

_____

_____

_____

EVERYDAY WINE

WINE & VINTAGE

Winemaker

Country & region

Where & when purchased   *Price*

Quantity & bottle size

Location

Comments

WINE & VINTAGE

Winemaker

Country & region

Where & when purchased   *Price*

Quantity & bottle size

Location

Comments

EVERYDAY WINE

WINE & VINTAGE

Winemaker

Country & region

Where & when purchased   *Price*

Quantity & bottle size

Location

Comments

WINE & VINTAGE

Winemaker

Country & region

Where & when purchased   *Price*

Quantity & bottle size

Location

Comments

EVERYDAY WINE

WINE & VINTAGE
_____

Winemaker
_____

Country & region
_____

Where & when purchased   _Price_
_____

Quantity & bottle size
_____

Location
_____

Comments
_____

_____

_____

_____

_____

WINE & VINTAGE
_____

Winemaker
_____

Country & region
_____

Where & when purchased   _Price_
_____

Quantity & bottle size
_____

Location
_____

Comments
_____

_____

_____

_____

_____

EVERYDAY WINE

WINE & VINTAGE

Winemaker

Country & region

Where & when purchased   *Price*

Quantity & bottle size

Location

Comments

WINE & VINTAGE

Winemaker

Country & region

Where & when purchased   *Price*

Quantity & bottle size

Location

Comments

EVERYDAY WINE

WINE & VINTAGE

Winemaker

Country & region

Where & when purchased   *Price*

Quantity & bottle size

Location

Comments

WINE & VINTAGE

Winemaker

Country & region

Where & when purchased   *Price*

Quantity & bottle size

Location

Comments

EVERYDAY WINE

WINE & VINTAGE

Winemaker

Country & region

Where & when purchased   *Price*

Quantity & bottle size

Location

Comments

WINE & VINTAGE

Winemaker

Country & region

Where & when purchased   *Price*

Quantity & bottle size

Location

Comments

EVERYDAY WINE

WINE & VINTAGE

Winemaker

Country & region

Where & when purchased   *Price*

Quantity & bottle size

Location

Comments

WINE & VINTAGE

Winemaker

Country & region

Where & when purchased   *Price*

Quantity & bottle size

Location

Comments

EVERYDAY WINE

WINE & VINTAGE

Winemaker

Country & region

Where & when purchased   Price

Quantity & bottle size

Location

Comments

WINE & VINTAGE

Winemaker

Country & region

Where & when purchased   Price

Quantity & bottle size

Location

Comments

EVERYDAY WINE

WINE & VINTAGE

Winemaker

Country & region

Where & when purchased   *Price*

Quantity & bottle size

Location

Comments

WINE & VINTAGE

Winemaker

Country & region

Where & when purchased   *Price*

Quantity & bottle size

Location

Comments

EVERYDAY WINE

WINE & VINTAGE

Winemaker

Country & region

Where & when purchased   Price

Quantity & bottle size

Location

Comments

WINE & VINTAGE

Winemaker

Country & region

Where & when purchased   Price

Quantity & bottle size

Location

Comments

EVERYDAY WINE

WINE & VINTAGE

Winemaker

Country & region

Where & when purchased   Price

Quantity & bottle size

Location

Comments

WINE & VINTAGE

Winemaker

Country & region

Where & when purchased   Price

Quantity & bottle size

Location

Comments

EVERYDAY WINE

WINE & VINTAGE

Winemaker

Country & region

Where & when purchased   _Price_

Quantity & bottle size

Location

Comments

WINE & VINTAGE

Winemaker

Country & region

Where & when purchased   _Price_

Quantity & bottle size

Location

Comments

EVERYDAY WINE

WINE & VINTAGE

Winemaker

Country & region

Where & when purchased   *Price*

Quantity & bottle size

Location

Comments

WINE & VINTAGE

Winemaker

Country & region

Where & when purchased   *Price*

Quantity & bottle size

Location

Comments

EVERYDAY WINE

WINE & VINTAGE

Winemaker

Country & region

Where & when purchased   *Price*

Quantity & bottle size

Location

Comments

WINE & VINTAGE

Winemaker

Country & region

Where & when purchased   *Price*

Quantity & bottle size

Location

Comments

EVERYDAY WINE

WINE & VINTAGE
_____

Winemaker
_____

Country & region
_____

Where & when purchased   _Price_
_____

Quantity & bottle size
_____

Location
_____

Comments
_____

_____

_____

_____

_____

WINE & VINTAGE
_____

Winemaker
_____

Country & region
_____

Where & when purchased   _Price_
_____

Quantity & bottle size
_____

Location
_____

Comments
_____

_____

_____

_____

_____

EVERYDAY WINE

WINE & VINTAGE

Winemaker

Country & region

Where & when purchased   Price

Quantity & bottle size

Location

Comments

WINE & VINTAGE

Winemaker

Country & region

Where & when purchased   Price

Quantity & bottle size

Location

Comments

EVERYDAY WINE

WINE & VINTAGE

Winemaker

Country & region

Where & when purchased   *Price*

Quantity & bottle size

Location

Comments

WINE & VINTAGE

Winemaker

Country & region

Where & when purchased   *Price*

Quantity & bottle size

Location

Comments

EVERYDAY WINE

WINE & VINTAGE

Winemaker

Country & region

Where & when purchased   *Price*

Quantity & bottle size

Location

Comments

WINE & VINTAGE

Winemaker

Country & region

Where & when purchased   *Price*

Quantity & bottle size

Location

Comments

EVERYDAY WINE

WINE & VINTAGE

Winemaker

Country & region

Where & when purchased   *Price*

Quantity & bottle size

Location

Comments

WINE & VINTAGE

Winemaker

Country & region

Where & when purchased   *Price*

Quantity & bottle size

Location

Comments

EVERYDAY WINE

WINE & VINTAGE
_____

Winemaker
_____

Country & region
_____

Where & when purchased   _Price_
_____

Quantity & bottle size
_____

Location
_____

Comments
_____
_____
_____
_____
_____
_____

WINE & VINTAGE
_____

Winemaker
_____

Country & region
_____

Where & when purchased   _Price_
_____

Quantity & bottle size
_____

Location
_____

Comments
_____
_____
_____
_____
_____
_____

EVERYDAY WINE

WINE & VINTAGE

Winemaker

Country & region

Where & when purchased   *Price*

Quantity & bottle size

Location

Comments

WINE & VINTAGE

Winemaker

Country & region

Where & when purchased   *Price*

Quantity & bottle size

Location

Comments

EVERYDAY WINE

WINE & VINTAGE

Winemaker

Country & region

Where & when purchased   *Price*

Quantity & bottle size

Location

Comments

WINE & VINTAGE

Winemaker

Country & region

Where & when purchased   *Price*

Quantity & bottle size

Location

Comments

EVERYDAY WINE

WINE & VINTAGE

Winemaker

Country & region

Where & when purchased   *Price*

Quantity & bottle size

Location

Comments

WINE & VINTAGE

Winemaker

Country & region

Where & when purchased   *Price*

Quantity & bottle size

Location

Comments

EVERYDAY WINE

WINE & VINTAGE

Winemaker

Country & region

Where & when purchased   *Price*

Quantity & bottle size

Location

Comments

WINE & VINTAGE

Winemaker

Country & region

Where & when purchased   *Price*

Quantity & bottle size

Location

Comments

188

EVERYDAY WINE

WINE & VINTAGE

Winemaker

Country & region

Where & when purchased   Price

Quantity & bottle size

Location

Comments

WINE & VINTAGE

Winemaker

Country & region

Where & when purchased   Price

Quantity & bottle size

Location

Comments

EVERYDAY WINE

WINE & VINTAGE

Winemaker

Country & region

Where & when purchased   *Price*

Quantity & bottle size

Location

Comments

WINE & VINTAGE

Winemaker

Country & region

Where & when purchased   *Price*

Quantity & bottle size

Location

Comments

EVERYDAY WINE

WINE & VINTAGE

Winemaker

Country & region

Where & when purchased   *Price*

Quantity & bottle size

Location

Comments

WINE & VINTAGE

Winemaker

Country & region

Where & when purchased   *Price*

Quantity & bottle size

Location

Comments

CREDITS

PHOTOGRAPHY CREDITS:

William Lingwood: pages 4 (Maison M. Chapoutier, Tain l'Hermitage & Châteauneuf-du-Pape, France), 10, 11, 14

Alan Williams: pages 8, 9, 13, 17, 19, 21, 23, 24, 26, 106, 108, 110

Francesca Yorke: page 12

Page 25 © Freixnet

ILLUSTRATION CREDITS:

Page 6 inset: courtesy of J.M. Chatelier

Page 7 inset: courtesy of Bonterra Vineyards

Pages 1, 3 inset, 79, 81, 83, 85, 87, 89, 91, 93, 95, 97, 99, 101, 103, 105, 113, 115, 117, 119, 121, 123, 125, 127, 129, 131, 133, 135, 137, 139, 141, 143, 145, 147, 149, 151, 153, 155, 193 below: all hand-drawings © Canicula 2012, under license of Shutterstock.com

Pages 156, 158, 160, 162, 164, 166, 168, 170, 172, 174, 176, 178, 180, 182, 184, 186, 188, 190: all hand-drawings © Dolly 2012, under license of Shutterstock.com

Pages 2, 3, 5, 15, 107 backgrounds © IndigoMoods / Alamy

Pages 2 inset, 32–77, 78, 80,82, 84 86, 88, 90, 92, 94, 96, 98, 100, 102, 104, 112, 114, 116, 118, 120, 122, 124, 126, 128, 130, 132, 134, 136, 138, 140, 142, 144, 146, 148, 150, 152, 154, 193 above: all hand-drawings © upstudio 2012, under license of Shutterstock.com

Pages 157, 159, 161, 163, 165, 167, 169, 171, 173, 175, 177, 179, 181, 183, 185, 187, 189, 191: all hand-drawings © zackblanton 2012, under license of Shutterstock.com